Original title:
Ashen Fragments Across the Faerie Crust

Copyright © 2025 Swan Charm

Author: Lan Donne
ISBN HARDBACK: 978-1-80559-334-8
ISBN PAPERBACK: 978-1-80559-833-6

# Surrendering Whispers to the Starlit Night

Under the velvet skies so deep,
Whispers of wishes gently sweep.
Stars twinkle with secrets to share,
In the silence, dreams linger there.

Moonlight dances on shadows cast,
Fleeting moments, hearts beating fast.
Every twinkle a story unfolds,
Promises whispered, the night unfolds.

Crickets sing in unison's call,
Nature's lullaby, a soothing thrall.
Breath of the night, tranquil and pure,
In its embrace, we find our cure.

Surrender to the beauty so vast,
Let the starlit dreams hold you fast.
In every silence, the echoes bright,
Lead us gently through the night.

Hearts entwined in celestial grace,
Lost in wonder, we find our place.
In the cosmos, our spirits unite,
Surrendering whispers to the night.

# Lurking Glories in the Shade of Enchantment

In the trees where shadows dwell,
Lurking glories weave their spell.
Whispers float on gentle breeze,
Secrets held by ancient trees.

Moonbeams waltz on leaves so green,
Glimmers hide where none have seen.
Every rustle, a tale untold,
Mysteries wrapped in shades of gold.

Creatures stir beneath the cloak,
In twilight's hush, they softly spoke.
What lies hidden, come seek and find,
Enchantment lingers, intertwined.

Through wild thickets, dreams take flight,
Chasing shadows in the night.
Nature's magic calls us near,
In this haven, we lose our fear.

With every step, the path unknown,
In the shade, the glories grown.
Bathed in wonder, the heart ignites,
Lurking glories in the night.

## Dreamlike Murmurs in Nature's Grasp

In twilight's embrace, whispers flow,
Leaves dance lightly, secrets bestow.
Moonbeams shimmer, a soft caress,
Nature's heartbeat, a gentle press.

Rippling waters hum a song,
Echoes of dreams where we belong.
Stars blink softly, guiding our way,
In nature's arms, we long to stay.

Petals flutter, a colorful breeze,
Carried by winds through the ancient trees.
Time pauses here, in serenity's clasp,
Lost in the moment, we softly grasp.

Whispers of night, cradled in dew,
Each breath a promise, a world anew.
Mysteries linger, in shadows they play,
In nature's hush, our spirits sway.

## Ethereal Dreams Among Forest Cinders

Through fog-kissed paths, shadows intertwine,
Whispers of magic in every line.
Cinders glimmer, a fire's fading glow,
As dreams awaken, the forest will grow.

Starlit canopies shelter our dreams,
Bathed in a softness, where nothing seems.
Each rustling branch tells a story old,
Hearts unite gently, in silence bold.

Moonlit cascades weave silver streams,
Reflecting our hopes, embracing our dreams.
In solitude's grasp, we find our way,
Embracing the night, welcoming day.

Footfalls echo, where echoes reside,
Woven in twilight, our fears subside.
Gentle caresses of winds through the trees,
Nature's own pulse, a sweet symphony.

# Flickering Memories in Dreamlike Landscapes

In hues of the sunset, memories gleam,
A tapestry woven from glimmers and dreams.
Each flicker ignites a story untold,
A journey through shadows, both tender and bold.

Wandering paths, where the wildflowers grow,
Brought forth by whispers of long-ago.
A heartbeat of echoes beneath the night sky,
Where glances linger, and soft sighs fly.

Beneath the vast arch, constellations shine,
Guiding our footsteps, your hand in mine.
Every ripple of water reflects a chance,
In this dreamscape, we sway and dance.

Soft breezes carry our laughter in flight,
Brushing the canvas, painting the night.
Moments entwined like threads of a seam,
A journey through time, wrapped in a dream.

## Love Letters Scattered in the Night

Underneath the blanket of starlit skies,
Whispers of love drift, igniting our sighs.
Letters of longing, penned in the dark,
Carried by winds, each word a spark.

With every heartbeat, the pages unfold,
Stories of passion, forever retold.
Moonlight reflects on the ink of our past,
A promise whispered, a love made to last.

In twilight's embrace, secrets we share,
Letters scattered gently, floating in air.
Each one a treasure, a fragment of time,
A chorus of voices, harmonious rhyme.

Stars are our witnesses, silent yet bright,
Holding our dreams through the velvet night.
Every word written, a part of the weave,
Love letters whisper what hearts dare believe.

## Mystical Echoes in the Twilight Thicket


In twilight's hush, where shadows loom,
Soft whispers dance, breaking the gloom.
Leaves murmur tales of the day's soft sigh,
As stars awaken in the velvet sky.

A gentle breeze stirs through the trees,
Carrying secrets on the evening's breeze.
Footsteps echo on a path untread,
Guided by dreams where spirits tread.

Moonlight weaves through branches bare,
Casting silhouettes of dreams laid bare.
Mystical echoes of the night unfold,
In the thicket where stories are told.

Creatures flit in the dusky light,
Cloaked in magic, soft and bright.
With every step, the night reveals,
The wondrous truth that twilight heals.

In this haven, time drifts slow,
As twilight whispers, soft and low.
Embrace the light in fading glow,
In mystical realms where dreams will flow.

# Gossamer Echoes in Shattered Light

Beyond the glass, where rainbows play,
Gossamer threads of light will sway.
Fractured beams of vibrant hues,
Whisper softly, share the news.

In the chaos, beauty glows,
With shattered light, the magic flows.
Every flicker tells a tale,
In the silence, shadows sail.

A tapestry of colors spun,
Where echoes of the past have run.
Each glimmer holds a story bright,
In the depths of the fading light.

Footprints trace the path of dreams,
In pools of light where nothing seems.
Gossamer echoes call us near,
In every shimmer, love appears.

Amidst the shards, we find our way,
Guided by light at the close of day.
In the dance of echoes, we unite,
Through gossamer threads in shattered light.

# The Veil of Glimmering Secrets

Behind the veil where whispers dwell,
Lies a trove, an untouched well.
Glimmers spark in hidden nooks,
Enticing hearts with forgotten books.

Secrets flutter like moths to flame,
Each one wrapped in a whispered name.
Through the shadows, the stories weave,
A dance of light, we dare believe.

In the twilight of our dreams anew,
The veil parts, revealing you.
With every secret held so tight,
A glimpse of magic, pure delight.

Mirrored truths in twilight's fold,
Glimmering softly, brave and bold.
The mysteries twine in a timeless thread,
As echoes of the past are spread.

In this realm of secrets kept,
Where silence lingers, dreams are swept.
The veil of glimmering secrets sighs,
With every heartbeat, truth defies.

# Radiant Vestiges Amongst the Fallen Leaves

In autumn's hush, where colors fade,
Radiant vestiges are displayed.
Leaves whisper tales with every fall,
Nature's canvas, a vibrant call.

Crimson, gold, and amber hues,
Amongst the fallen, memories fuse.
Each rustling leaf sings serenades,
Of time's embrace in the cool glades.

Beneath the boughs, the whispers low,
Echoing warmth in the chill below.
The ground adorned in twilight's dress,
Holds stories of laughter, love, and sadness.

Amongst the leaves, where dreams reside,
The secrets of the forest hide.
Radiant shadows, soft and bright,
Illuminate paths in fading light.

With every step, the past reveals,
The radiant truth that nature feels.
In tangled roots and branches weaves,
The sacred bond amidst the leaves.

# Whispers of Light Beneath the Wistful Sky

With every dawn the shadows fade,
The light creeps in, a gentle shade.
It wraps around the waking trees,
A lullaby upon the breeze.

Beneath the skies of azure blue,
The whispers float, they're soft and true.
Each ray a secret yet untold,
In golden threads, the dreams unfold.

Where mountains rise and rivers flow,
The dance of light begins to show.
In fields adorned with morning dew,
The world awakens, bright and new.

A canvas painted, hue by hue,
Nature's brush, with strokes so true.
In every corner, magic gleams,
As daylight brews the sweetest dreams.

The sun ascends, a radiant glow,
In every heart, the hope will grow.
Whispers of light, a soft reply,
Beneath the vast and wistful sky.

# Shadows Breathing in a Realm of Wonder

In twilight's hush, the shadows play,
They dance in whispers, drift away.
A realm of wonder, dark entwined,
With secrets kept, the heart aligned.

Beneath the stars, they softly weave,
A tapestry that dares believe.
Each echo twirls in moonlit streams,
Awakening the lostest dreams.

The night unfurls its velvet cloak,
As dreams unfurl, in silence spoke.
With every breath, the magic swells,
In hidden realms where beauty dwells.

In quiet woods where starlights gleam,
The shadows sigh, as if to dream.
They breathe the night, a soft embrace,
A world transformed, a hidden place.

With every blink, the mind will roam,
In shadows found, we find our home.
A whisper here, a glimpse of grace,
In this realm, we find our place.

# Fragments of Flight in the Nettle Boughs

Amidst the boughs, the fleeting flight,
A songbird's call, a pure delight.
In rustling leaves, the whispers blend,
As nature's stories gently mend.

Fragments of dreams in morning light,
Can stretch the heart and take to flight.
In every glance, the world unfolds,
With tales of life the forest holds.

With skies aglow and spirits high,
The nettles sway, and so do I.
Each rustle heard, each breath a sign,
In nature's hands, all souls entwine.

A dance of color, winged embrace,
In every fork, the wild will chase.
The joy of flight, both fierce and free,
In tangled boughs we cease to be.

Every moment, a fleeting spark,
In silence shared, we leave our mark.
Fly gently forth, dear dreams of mine,
In fragments found, our lives align.

# The Cradle of Dreams and Shattered Stars

In shadows cast by fleeting light,
The cradle holds both day and night.
With dreams in hand, we softly sway,
And whisper hopes that guide our way.

The stars above, they shine so bright,
Yet some may fall, lost to the night.
In every gleam, a spark remains,
Where shattered hopes bring joyful gains.

A tapestry of wishes spun,
In cosmic threads, we all are one.
The cradle rocks, both calm and fierce,
In every heart, the dreams immerse.

Out in the dark, they seek their place,
The fallen stars, a fleeting grace.
With each new dawn, the past will blend,
To cradled dreams that never end.

In silence found, the universe sighs,
As new stars bloom in endless skies.
The cradle swings, though shadows may,
It holds our dreams, our night, our day.

# Shattered Illusions and Glittering Ash

In the dusk of dreams that fade,
Whispers twirl in shadowed glade.
Memories weave a fragile dance,
Caught in fate's unyielding trance.

Fragments fall like autumn leaves,
Scarred by truths the heart deceives.
Glimmers shine in ashen grey,
Hope, a spark in disarray.

Echoes stir in silent night,
Flickering with fleeting light.
Visions shatter, yet they gleam,
Life's a haunting, fragile dream.

Longing threads the woven air,
Threads that tug with secret care.
In the ashes, embers glow,
From the past, new paths will grow.

## Veils of Light in the Withered Grove

Amidst the leaves, where shadows sigh,
Veils of light flicker, soft and high.
Whispers of the forest deep,
Secrets that the ancients keep.

Bark and stone, with time they blend,
Tales of old that never end.
Golden hues through branches weave,
In the still, we start to believe.

Dancing glimmers, kind and sweet,
Nature's pulse beneath our feet.
Peaceful echoes, rustling song,
In this grove, we all belong.

Hands of time reach out and trace,
Life's connections, nature's grace.
Veils of light, with colors spun,
Woven threads of many one.

# Twilight Echoes of Enchanted Fragments

In twilight's hush, the world concedes,
Shrieks of night drown in soft needs.
Fragments of a thousand dreams,
Whirl through time in silver beams.

Moonlight dances on the dew,
Painting whispers, bright and true.
Stars awaken, ancient lore,
Echoes of what came before.

Voices rise on evening air,
Songs of hope, and of despair.
Heartbeats thrum like woven threads,
In the calm, the spirit spreads.

Every shadow, every spark,
Guides us gently through the dark.
Enchanted fragments weave the night,
In this mist, our souls take flight.

# Celestial Remnants in the Faery Mist

In faery mist, the twilight gleams,
Celestial remnants, woven dreams.
Stardust drapes on every tree,
Whispers from the galaxy.

Softly shining, glows the night,
With each breath, the stars invite.
Wings of wonder brush the air,
In the silence, magic's there.

Echoes pulse like beating hearts,
Drawing us from worlds apart.
Remnants of the cosmic dance,
In this realm, we take our chance.

Underneath the velvet sky,
Dreams set sail and hopes can fly.
In the mist, the spirits play,
Guiding souls along the way.

# Specters of Light and Dark

In the hush of night's embrace,
Shadows flicker, leave their trace.
Whispers dance on moonlit sands,
Time slips through ethereal hands.

Eclipsed dreams in silence soar,
Glimmers behind every door.
Light entwines with shadows' play,
In this realm where spirits sway.

Wanderers lost in twilight's grace,
Search for warmth in a cold place.
Echoed voices, soft and near,
Guide the way with whispered cheer.

In the depths, a fleeting spark,
Life and death leave their mark.
Through the dark, we seek the bright,
Specters twist in soft moonlight.

# Shimmering Embers in the Sylvan Air

Golden leaves that softly sway,
Catch the sun in bright array.
Nature's breath, a sweet refrain,
Embers dance in daylight's gain.

Whispers trail through woodland glades,
Morning's light, a gentle shade.
Fireflies flicker, pure delight,
In the weave of fading night.

Crystal streams with stories lie,
Beneath the vast and open sky.
Roots and branches intertwine,
In this realm, the world's divine.

Every sound, a heartbeat true,
Carried by the winds that blew.
Life ignites in every nook,
Shimmering glows in every book.

Night falls soft, the stars appear,
Embers whisper, drawing near.
Sylvan air, a tranquil song,
In their warmth, we all belong.

# Wisps of Desire in the Smoky Delve

In the cave where shadows dwell,
Secrets held by flames that swell.
Warmth escapes from tender sighs,
Desire flickers in the rise.

Wraiths of passion linger near,
Every heartbeat crystal clear.
In the smoke, dreams intertwine,
Pulling threads, both yours and mine.

Amid the haze, we seek a flame,
Fueling hearts without a name.
Glimmers tease from every wall,
Wisps of longing, rise and fall.

Candles flicker, wax drips slow,
Love ignites in the warm glow.
Find me here in the embrace,
In the depths of this sacred space.

Eager souls, we chase the fire,
Every glance ignites desire.
In this delve, let passions weave,
Together, we shall believe.

# Chasing Luminescence in the Fading Light

As the day begins to wane,
Shadows stretch across the lane.
Colors fade to softest gray,
Chasing light before it's day.

Glimmers trail through twilight's veil,
Echoes of a whispered tale.
Every breath a fleeting sigh,
Chasing dreams that dare to fly.

In this moment, hearts ignite,
Fates entwine in fading light.
Golden hues of dusk entice,
Holding on, we pay the price.

Threads of silver, paths align,
In this dance, our souls entwine.
Steps may falter, yet we strive,
For with love, we feel alive.

As the stars begin to peek,
Softly, tender words we speak.
Chasing luminescence bold,
As the night begins to hold.

# Shards of Echoes Among the Starlit Thorns

Silent whispers dance through night,
Amidst the thorns, a hidden light.
Shards of echoes, softly bled,
A symphony of words unsaid.

Winds carry tales of lost delight,
As starlit dreams take fragile flight.
Each sparkle tells a secret true,
In night's embrace, they weave anew.

Nature sighs beneath the gaze,
Of silver moons in twilight's haze.
With every thorn, a story weaves,
A tapestry of hopes and leaves.

The sky reflects our weary fight,
While shadows blend with dawn's first light.
In every shard, a memory stays,
Among the thorns, where silence plays.

Let echoes linger, softly hum,
Through starlit paths where feelings come.
In this realm of twinkling fate,
Let dreams unfurl, never too late.

# Twinkling Bits of Forgotten Dreams

In the corners of the mind's eye,
Twinkling bits start to comply.
Forgotten dreams, both bright and rare,
A dance of hope in evening air.

Whispers of what could have been,
Glimmers lost, yet shared within.
Each bit a tale, a hidden spark,
Illuminates the fading dark.

Time weaves threads of muted gold,
In every heartbeat, stories told.
Yet shadows grasp what can't sustain,
As dreams dissolve, like fleeting rain.

With gentle hands, we gather light,
Brushing against the grip of night.
In every twinkle, shadows gleam,
A chorus born from hearts that dream.

Awake, arise, let visions soar,
In the depths, find something more.
Twinkling bits will guide the way,
To lands where hope and courage play.

# Reflections in the City of Shadows

Amidst the streets, where echoes blend,
Reflections dance, they twist and bend.
City of shadows, deep and wide,
Hiding truths that often slide.

Mirrored faces, stories caged,
Every glance a heart engaged.
In twilight's hold, they silently speak,
Of dreams pursued and futures bleak.

Beneath the streetlamps, secrets sigh,
Lost in the noise, they float and fly.
Each spark of life a fleeting glance,
A moment lost in a shadowed dance.

Yet through the dim, a light emerges,
Breaking forth like daring urges.
In the city where echoes roam,
Each reflection finds its way back home.

Step by step, we chase the fate,
In shadows thick, we hesitate.
Yet through the night, hope always glows,
In reflections of the city's throes.

# Fractured Realities in Misty Meadows

In misty meadows, dreams collide,
Fractured truths that we can't hide.
Softly veiled in twilight's breath,
Life's gentle touch, a dance with death.

Among the flowers, whispers trace,
Stories linger in each space.
The fog reveals what lies beneath,
A fragile world, both light and sheath.

With every step, illusions rise,
The heartbeats drum like distant cries.
Misty shadows cradle the light,
Guiding souls through the haunting night.

Yet in the fractures, beauty seems,
To stitch together broken dreams.
Each dew-kissed petal, a tender heart,
Whispers of worlds that never part.

So wander through this haunting ground,
Where truths once lost can still be found.
In meadows shrouded, love will sing,
A symphony of remembering.

# Glimmers of Hope Through Veils of Mist

In the embrace of dawn's soft light,
Whispers of dreams take gentle flight.
Shadows fade as colors blend,
A promise of hope that will not end.

Misty tendrils weave through trees,
Carrying secrets in a breeze.
Glimmers dance on dew-kissed grass,
Reminding us that moments pass.

Through the fog, a path appears,
Guiding us through ancient fears.
Each step forward, a heart set free,
In a world where we choose to be.

With every breath, we rise and stand,
Painting futures with a steady hand.
In the silence, strength we find,
Glimmers of hope, forever kind.

## Starlit Whispers in the Forgotten Glade

Beneath the canopy of ancient trees,
Whispers flow on a gentle breeze.
Stars above flicker like a sigh,
In the glade where dreams lie shy.

Moonlight spills on the forest floor,
Each shadow speaks of days before.
Crickets sing a lullaby sweet,
A melody where hearts can meet.

Here in the silence, spirits roam,
In this secret, they find their home.
Starlit paths lead to the unknown,
Invisible threads, ties we've sown.

Memories linger like a soft embrace,
In this haven, our souls find grace.
Lost in the magic, time stands still,
In the glade, we bend to will.

### Celestial Debris Beneath Gnarled Branches

Caught in the web of a twilight sky,
Stars descend as night draws nigh.
Beneath the branches, broken dreams,
Drift on the ground where silence seems.

Fragments of light fall softly down,
Adorning the earth like a ghostly crown.
In the shadows, echoes linger near,
A symphony of thoughts we hold dear.

Gnarled fingers stretch toward the vast,
Chasing whispers of a time long past.
Celestial debris, a wondrous sight,
Guides our hearts through the endless night.

Rustling leaves tell tales untold,
Of courage, love, and hearts bold.
Here we gather the scattered seeds,
In the hush, the spirit feeds.

# Dreams Woven in a Tapestry of Shadows

In twilight's glow, shadows entwine,
Weaving dreams in a design divine.
Threads of silver, whispers in night,
Crafting visions that take flight.

Each stitch tells a story brave,
Of hopes ignited, paths we crave.
In the fabric, colors play,
Bringing forth the dawn of day.

Within the shadows, visions bloom,
Filling hearts with life and room.
A tapestry rich with every shade,
Capturing moments that never fade.

As we wander through this art,
Each heartbeat reflects a part.
Dreams woven close, forever spun,
In the dance of shadows, we are one.

## Fractals of Light in Gossamer Shadows

Through the twilight, whispers call,
Fleeting glimmers, shadows fall.
Colors dance, a soft embrace,
Fractals bloom in hidden space.

Resonating with a silent chord,
Nature's secrets, softly stored.
Light refracts and bends with grace,
Gossamer threads, a dreamlike trace.

In the stillness, patterns weave,
A tapestry, none perceive.
Each reflection speaks of time,
In fractals, rhythm, and rhyme.

# The Chorus of Shadows on Ethereal Wings

In twilight's grasp, they softly sing,
Echoes of night on whispering wing.
A chorus swells beneath the stars,
Shadows dance, like fleeting scars.

Sculpted dreams in twilight's haze,
Mingling softly, lost in a daze.
Ethereal movements, wild and free,
Shadows chant in harmony.

As moonlight drapes the silent earth,
They share their stories, birth to birth.
A timeless song where silence reigns,
The chorus weaves through joy and pains.

# Glimmers Through the Misty Barricade

Veils of vapor, softly rolled,
Glimmers shine, their stories told.
Eager hands reach for the light,
Through the mist, hope takes flight.

Each shimmer hides a distant tale,
In shadows cast, the dreams set sail.
Fleeting moments, eternity's thread,
Through barricades, visions spread.

Awakening hearts in stillness crave,
A glimpse of what the world once gave.
Through the veil, a path is paved,
Glimmers guide the souls once braved.

# Traces of Luster in Forgotten Paths

Amidst the ruins, whispers sigh,
Traces linger, as time goes by.
Luster shines where shadows creep,
In forgotten paths, secrets sleep.

Every step, a story shared,
Lost in echoes, dreams once bared.
Glimmers guide the winds of fate,
Through ancient trails we contemplate.

In twilight's glow, memories fuse,
The past ignites the heart's muse.
Traces of light in paths unwalked,
Ancient whispers, forever talked.

# The Lilt of Shattered Whimsy

In dreams where laughter used to glide,
The echoes play, a hidden tide.
Beneath the stars, we lost our way,
Yet still, we dance till break of day.

With every whimsy, shattered light,
We find our paths in dark of night.
Fractured hopes weave through the air,
A ballet spun from whispered care.

Where once the joy held sway and held,
Now gentle sighs by silence felled.
Yet in the shards, new colors bloom,
A spark ignites, dispelling gloom.

So let the lilt of fleeting dreams,
Guide us through life's swirling schemes.
From broken pieces, life's sweet song,
In every heart, we still belong.

As shadows fade, and dawn ascends,
We gather life's ephemeral bends.
With brave resolve, we'll chase the light,
In every jest, a strength ignites.

# Dusk's Embrace and Silken Ash

In twilight's hush, the world unwinds,
Soft whispers trace the evening winds.
As day concedes to night's warm charm,
The silken ash holds dreams, so calm.

Embers flicker on the sable sky,
Where memories linger, not goodbye.
Each star a tale of love and fate,
As shadows blend, we contemplate.

The crescent moon, a watchful eye,
Bestows its glow as night drifts by.
In dusk's embrace, our worries fade,
With every breath, a serenade.

We wander through the starlit haze,
Where silence sings of ancient ways.
An ethereal dance upon the grass,
In this soft shroud, our spirits pass.

In whispered dreams, we'll softly tread,
Through paths of twilight, gently led.
In silence found, we find release,
In dusk's embrace, we seek our peace.

# Chimeric Flutters of Starlit Dust

In shadows cast by dreams untold,
Chimeras flutter, bright and bold.
With wings of starlit dust, they play,
In realms where night and magic sway.

They dance upon the silver beams,
Unraveling the fabric of dreams.
Each twist and turn, a story spun,
Beneath the moon, we become one.

Where echoes twine with fate's sweet thread,
In whispered hues of ardent red.
The night unfolds its mysteries,
As time suspends and worries cease.

Through realms of wonder, we embark,
On journeys led by blazing spark.
These chimeric flutters, wild and free,
Hold echoes of eternity.

With every step, our spirits soar,
In starlit dust, we find our core.
Each fleeting moment, deftly spun,
All paths converge, no need to run.

# Whispers of the Enchanted Ember

In twilight's glow, the embers sing,
Of ancient tales where shadows cling.
With whispered hopes, our dreams take flight,
In realms where day yields to the night.

The fire flickers, casting spells,
Each glow a secret that it tells.
From every spark, a story wakes,
In rhythm with the heart that aches.

The night enfolds its velvet grace,
A tender shield, a warm embrace.
In every shadow, light will grow,
Through whispered winds, the embers flow.

We gather close, the warmth to share,
In every glance, a longing stare.
The magic lingers, soft and sweet,
In every pulse, our lives complete.

So let the whispers guide us home,
Where every ember starts to roam.
In every breath, a wish bestowed,
The enchanted ember, our hearts' abode.

## Whims of the Fae in Stars and Shadows

In twilight's whisper, fae wings unfurl,
They dance on beams of starlit pearl.
With laughter light, they weave a spell,
In shadows deep, their secrets dwell.

Moonlit paths where dreams take flight,
In silver mist, they greet the night.
With gossamer threads, they stitch the dark,
In gentle breezes, hear their spark.

Beneath the trees, where silence sings,
Fae stories float on magic's wings.
Through dappled glades, their laughter streams,
In every heart, they plant their dreams.

As dawn approaches, they fade away,
Yet leave behind hints of their play.
In each soft rustle, a promise lies,
Their whimsy caught in starlit skies.

So dance, dear soul, in twilight's clasp,
Embrace the dreams that fae enwrap.
For in the night, where shadows blend,
Whims of the fae will never end.

# The Art of Secrets in the Silvered Grove

In the silvered grove, where shadows creep,
Secrets linger; they're ours to keep.
With twilight's brush, the night unfurls,
A tapestry of whispered worlds.

Beneath the trees, where silence reigns,
Hidden wonders fill the veins.
Each rustling leaf, a tale to tell,
In the heart of darkness, secrets dwell.

Sprinkled stardust on the ground,
Echoes of dreams in silence found.
With every step, the secrets breathe,
A silent pact, we weave and sheathe.

In moonlight's glow, truths softly gleam,
Guarded whispers in a dreamer's dream.
From gentle winds to shadows wide,
The art of secrets we won't abide.

So tread with care in this sacred space,
For every secret has its place.
In the silvered grove, let joy arise,
Each secret blooms 'neath starlit skies.

# Dappled Echoes in Fae-Drenched Dreams

In dreams adorned with fae's embrace,
The dappled echoes find their place.
Among the leaves, in soft moonlight,
Their laughter lingers, pure delight.

Through fae-drenched fields, we wander free,
With every step, a melody.
Each whispering breeze, a fleeting thought,
In dreams of wonder, never caught.

The sweet perfume of night unfolds,
A story in the silence holds.
With every twirl, the shadows play,
Dappled echoes lead the way.

In twilight's glow, our spirits soar,
With fae as guides, we're evermore.
Through realms unseen, on magic beams,
We find our paths in layered dreams.

So let your heart in whispers blend,
As dappled echoes never end.
For in the night where fae take flight,
Our dreams are etched in purest light.

# Sacred Light on Veiled Abandon

In veiled abandon, hearts ignite,
With sacred light, we chase the night.
In shadows cast by whispered glows,
The quiet truth of love bestows.

Through tangled woods, we roam as one,
With every step, a new dawn's spun.
In glimmers bright, our spirits rise,
Sacred light beneath darkened skies.

In secret moments, time suspends,
Where laughter lives, and warmth extends.
With every sigh, the night unfolds,
A tale of magic yet untold.

Through veils of mist, our dreams take flight,
In blissful dance, we paint the night.
Hand in hand, we chase the dawn,
A world awakened, veils withdrawn.

So let us weave this sacred path,
In light and love, escape the wrath.
For in the night's sweet, soft embrace,
Veiled abandon gives dreams their space.

# Whispers of Charred Stardust

Beneath the night, where shadows flow,
Lost secrets dance with the stars' glow.
In ashes bright, a tale is spun,
Whispers echo, the day is done.

Flickers fade in the cosmic breeze,
Hearts ablaze with forgotten pleas.
Fragments fall like fleeting light,
Carried softly into the night.

Silent wonders in the vast expanse,
Dreams collide in a twilight trance.
From charred remains, new worlds arise,
As stardust fades, we learn to rise.

In cosmic realms, our spirits soar,
Beyond the veil, we seek for more.
Through whispers lost in timeless hymn,
Woven together at the world's rim.

So take my hand beneath this sky,
Where charred stardust will never die.
In every breath, we find our tune,
Together bound, beneath the moon.

# Luminous Shards of Enchantment

In twilight's grasp, we find our spark,
Luminous shards ignite the dark.
With every glimmer, dreams unfold,
Enchanting stories yet untold.

We wander paths of silver light,
In gentle whispers of the night.
Magic stirs in the quiet air,
Dancing softly without a care.

Woven threads of midnight's gold,
Nurtured secrets waiting to be told.
Through each shimmer, we reach for more,
As the universe opens its door.

With every pulse, enchantment breathes,
In the heart's core, a promise weaves.
Caught in the web of dreams so bright,
We become stardust, lost in flight.

Together we chase the fleeting gleam,
Living within the edge of a dream.
In luminous shards, our spirits rise,
Reflecting magic in the skies.

# Echoes in the Gossamer Shadows

In whispers soft, the shadows play,
Echoes linger where night meets day.
Gossamer threads weave tales of yore,
In unseen realms, we seek to explore.

Through twilight paths, we softly tread,
Where echoes whisper of things unsaid.
The veil thins where secrets glance,
Inviting souls to join the dance.

Each step a story in fragile light,
In shadow's realm, we take our flight.
With every heartbeat, truth unfolds,
In gossamer dreams, we become bold.

Silhouettes of hope in dusky haze,
Lost in the beauty of fleeting days.
In every echo, a promise glows,
Illuminating where the heart knows.

So tread with care in the night's embrace,
Find solace in shadows, a sacred space.
Gossamer whispers will guide your way,
Through echoes ancient, forever stay.

# Broken Dreams on Velvet Wings

On velvet wings, we start to soar,
Broken dreams whisper at the door.
Each flutter a sigh, where hopes align,
In the silence, their shadows entwine.

Fragments of light in the dusky air,
Haunting echoes of dreams laid bare.
With every heartbeat, they softly sing,
Messages lost on fragile wing.

In twilight's grace, we find our strength,
Celebrating love at arm's length.
Though dreams may break, we rise anew,
On velvet wings, our spirits flew.

Through storms endured, we carry on,
In search of dawn, the night is gone.
With every failure, new flight begins,
On heart's horizon, where freedom spins.

So trust the journey, let fears take flight,
In broken dreams, there lies the light.
On velvet wings, we will defend,
The beauty found in how we mend.

# Twilit Raindrops on Forgotten Paths

Twilit raindrops fall like dreams,
Whispering softly through the trees,
Each drop a tale of shadowed night,
Merging paths where silence breathes.

Crimson leaves dance in the gloom,
Winding trails of dampened lore,
Footsteps echo where souls once trod,
Forgotten paths forevermore.

Moonlight kisses the pebbled stones,
Reflecting stars with gentle grace,
As twilight weaves through ghosts of life,
In every heart, a secret place.

The breeze carries a longing sigh,
Where memories linger in the mist,
Raindrops shimmer, clear as love,
In the twilight, they softly twist.

Here in the hush, the world awakes,
Each droplet sings a fleeting song,
Through the paths where shadows dwell,
Twilit raindrops, where dreams belong.

# Everlasting Echoes Within Leafy Haunts

In leafy haunts of emerald green,
Whispers float on gentle air,
Echoes of laughter, soft and sweet,
Lost in the dreams, forever rare.

Sunlight filters through the trees,
Painting shadows on the ground,
As time stands still no echoes fade,
Within the woods, a peace profound.

Every rustle, every sigh,
Holds the essence of the past,
Memories linger in the boughs,
In tangled roots, they hold steadfast.

Nature sings a timeless song,
In harmony with beating hearts,
Each note a thread of life's embrace,
Within the forest, hope imparts.

Everlasting echoes linger here,
In leafy sanctuaries so close,
Where every moment weaves a tale,
Of whispered love and gentle prose.

## The Music of Shadows in Faerie Glens

In faerie glens where shadows play,
The music swells with ancient sound,
Melodies spin from whispered leaves,
As twilight drapes the night around.

The brook hums softly, gliding by,
In harmony with twilight's glow,
Each note a glimpse of magic's dream,
Where time flows gently, soft and slow.

Fairy lights dance on dewy grass,
Casting spells of luminescent glee,
As creatures twirl in silent joy,
Swaying to the night's reverie.

Beneath the boughs of ancient oaks,
The shadows play their secret game,
With every breeze that curls and bends,
The music calls, yet none can tame.

In faerie glens, the hearts take flight,
Where shadows sing and dreams entice,
The music lingers, soft and bright,
In night's embrace, it whispers twice.

## Eclipsed Whispers Beneath Silken Skies

Eclipsed whispers beneath the stars,
Float gently on the velvet night,
Tales of love that softly weave,
Through silken skies, where dreams take flight.

Moonlit glow on serene waters,
Reflects the shadows of the past,
Each ripple holds a fleeting word,
In whispered tones, the memories cast.

Darkened clouds drift lazily by,
Enfolding secrets, lost in time,
Every sigh a story shared,
In twilight's breath, a perfect rhyme.

The night wraps all in tender hush,
As echoes fade to softest grace,
Beneath the heavens' jeweled cloak,
Eclipsed whispers find their place.

Here in the quiet, love's refrain,
Whispers linger, sweet and shy,
In the stillness of the night air,
Beneath the canvas of starlit sky.

# Mystical Shards in Twilight's Grasp

In twilight's embrace, the shadows dance,
Whispers of magic in every chance.
Shards of light in soft decay,
Glimmers fading, lost to day.

Echoes linger where dreams once rose,
Winds carry secrets, as twilight knows.
In this realm where silence sings,
Mystical realms wear unseen rings.

Stars awaken with silver tears,
Bathing the night in timeless years.
Paths untrodden, stories untold,
In twilight's grasp, the world unfolds.

Glimpses of lovers in the breeze,
Shimmering hopes like fluttering leaves.
Each moment captured, a fleeting glance,
In twilight's heart, we find our chance.

As shadows deep, the night ascends,
With every beat, a story bends.
Mystical shards, a soft embrace,
In twilight's hold, we find our place.

## Elysian Traces in the Soft Twilight

In twilight's glow, the heavens sigh,
Elysian traces in the sky.
Colors blend in soft delight,
Painting dreams, igniting night.

Gentle breezes whisper near,
Carrying echoes of love so clear.
Footprints woven on the ground,
In soft twilight, lost dreams found.

Leaves rustle with ancient songs,
Melodies telling where one belongs.
Elysian paths, both dark and bright,
Guide the heart through the veiled night.

Stars peep shyly, one by one,
Heralding the night, the day is done.
Memory dances in the air,
Soft twilight holds the world with care.

Each breath taken, a moment of grace,
In twilight's arms, we find our place.
Elysian whispers, serene and fine,
In the soft twilight, your hand in mine.

# Soft Echoes in the Glistening Woods

In the woods where secrets sleep,
Soft echoes in the silence creep.
Glistening leaves with dewdrops bright,
Whispering tales in the dimming light.

Mossy paths where shadows play,
Guide lost souls in their gentle sway.
Each rustle tells of night's embrace,
In the woods, we find our space.

Moonlight dances on water's face,
Reflections weave a tender grace.
Soft echoes, a symphony sweet,
Nature's heartbeat, a rhythmic beat.

Stars twinkle through the leafy dome,
Soft murmurs call the woods their home.
In each breath, the magic flows,
In glistening woods, the spirit knows.

Every shadow tells its tale,
In the woods where whispers sail.
Soft echoes, like a lover's sigh,
In the glistening woods, dreams never die.

## Ethereal Dust in Fae-Draped Whispers

Ethereal dust on the cool night air,
Fae-draped whispers linger everywhere.
In fragile dreams where we take flight,
Mysteries bloom in the soft starlight.

Glimmers of laughter, haunting the night,
Dancing shadows in silver light.
Every sigh a tale to tell,
In the realm where fae spirits dwell.

Beneath the moon's enchanting glow,
Secrets flow with the river's flow.
Ethereal dust like a painter's stroke,
In whispers soft, forgotten yoke.

Through the night, the fae weave spells,
In tangled dreams where magic dwells.
Every heartbeat, a memory spun,
In ethereal dust, we are one.

In these realms where light and dark meet,
Fae-draped whispers, a soft heartbeat.
Ethereal dust, our guiding light,
In whispers calm, we embrace the night.

# Shadows Cast by the Broken Moon

In the stillness of the night,
Whispers dance with the light.
Moonbeams weave a tale of woe,
Casting shadows on the snow.

A figure cloaked in dark despair,
Haunted by what once was fair.
The silence shrieks a mournful tune,
Lost within the broken moon.

Stars flicker in their distant flight,
Sowing dreams in the velvet night.
Yet, beneath the silver glow,
Lie secrets that none may know.

Ghostly echoes of the past,
Whisper truths that fade too fast.
In the darkness, fears resume,
Yet hope lingers 'neath the moon.

With each heartbeat, shadows grow,
A dance of memories and sorrow.
Yet in the quiet, strength will bloom,
Amidst the shadows of the moon.

# Celestial Echoes in the Fae's Lament

Deep within the ancient glade,
Fae of light and dark parade.
With dulcet tones they sing of loss,
Their hearts, a heavy weight to toss.

Leaves shimmer with a silver hue,
Echoes chant of dreams anew.
Yet shadows weave with every sound,
In this realm where pain is found.

The stars above weep gentle tears,
As night unveils their hidden fears.
Each note a sigh, each dance a plea,
In the realm of the wild and free.

Misty veils of time entwine,
Bringing forth a fate divine.
Yet in this magic lies the strife,
In every heart, a hint of life.

Elders speak in haunted verse,
Of choices made and paths diverse.
In glimmers bright, their hopes ignite,
Yet shadows linger, dimming light.

## Glimmers of Lost Time in Gossamer Fields

In fields where time and dreams collide,
Fragile whispers softly bide.
Each gust of wind tells tales of yore,
Echoes linger, forevermore.

Golden grains sway in the breeze,
Carried whispers from the trees.
Gossamer threads weave stories tight,
Of moments lost in fading light.

Stars twinkle through the twilight sky,
Reminders of days gone awry.
Yet in the stillness, hope prevails,
As magic dances, never pales.

Among the blooms, there lies a spark,
A beacon shining in the dark.
Each petal holds a secret lost,
Of love regained, no matter the cost.

Fleeting memories tread so near,
While silence sings a song of cheer.
In gossamer fields, time bends,
For every start must find its ends.

# Remnants of Light in the Hollow Grove

In the hollow where shadows dwell,
Remnants of light weave a spell.
Each flicker, bright against the gray,
Guides the lost upon their way.

Trees whisper secrets of the night,
Holding close the fading light.
Branches sway, a soft embrace,
In this solemn, sacred place.

The moon hangs low, a watchful eye,
As time drifts gently, like a sigh.
In the grove where silence flows,
A promise lingers, gently grows.

Stars peep through the canopy wide,
A celestial path, they'll guide.
Though shadows creep, hope remains,
Remnants of light, love's sweet gains.

Through the night, hearts softly beat,
In this grove where shadows meet.
With every breath, the warmth will bloom,
Among the remnants in the gloom.

# Remnants of a Dreaming Realm

In shadows soft where secrets fall,
A tapestry of twilight calls.
Whispers dance on whispered breath,
Echoes lingering past sweet death.

Beneath the stars, a river gleams,
Where every heart still weaves its dreams.
The night unfolds, a velvet seam,
Elysian tales of the silent stream.

Lost in the haze of silver night,
Glimmers of truth in fleeting flight.
Fragments swirling, memories bright,
Bathed in the glow of soft starlight.

A canvas spun in hues untold,
Where time itself feels soft and bold.
Embracing all, the lost, the found,
In realms where ancient spirits sound.

The wildflowers sway with the breeze,
While moonlit paths lead where hearts seize.
In every sigh, the past resounds,
In remnants of love that's wrapped in bounds.

# Surreal Echoes of the Sylph's Breath

Softly gliding through leafy shades,
A sylph awakens, nature fades.
In the twilight, she begins her flight,
Weaving magic in the fading light.

With the breath of winds that sing,
She dances lightly, whispers ring.
Circling through the hollowed trees,
In every pause, the world believes.

Echoes stretch 'neath crescent moons,
Cradling dreams in softest tunes.
Every flicker, a fleeting trace,
Of whispering shadows in timeless space.

Through misty realms where visions flow,
The sylphs of night begin to glow.
In a maze of desires, lost and found,
Their ethereal presence, a silent sound.

Breath of the night, so pure and clear,
Rising echoes, all that we fear.
In surreal hues, their essence blends,
Awakening hearts, where magic sends.

# Flickers in a Darkened Glade

Amidst the trees, a flicker glows,
Where twilight whispers, silence grows.
A glade wrapped softly in shadow's veil,
Each breath a moment, a timeless tale.

Fireflies dart in a madcap dance,
Twinkling lights in a fleeting glance.
Here the air is thick with dreams,
Weaving through fire's tender beams.

The stillness weaves a tapestry,
Of whispered thoughts and reverie.
Underneath the ancient boughs,
A tranquil heart still makes its vows.

Shadows stretch with the sinking sun,
Embracing all that's lost, all's begun.
An echo lingers from distant streams,
In the glade where the lost dream.

Crickets sing in the near twilight,
Nature leaves a mark with every flight.
In every flicker, a story spins,
Of laughter, love, and where it begins.

# The Dusk Linger of Whispers and Dreams

At dusk's embrace, where whispers dwell,
A realm emerges with stories to tell.
In fading light, the secrets bloom,
Enfolding hearts in shadowed room.

With every breath, a tale unwinds,
Echoes of love, the heart it finds.
Dreams linger softly on whispering sight,
Woven through the fabric of night.

The horizon blushes, a canvas grey,
Where day's remnants gently sway.
Image of thoughts, now far and wide,
In dusk's caress, the heart confides.

In tranquil songs that nature hums,
The pulse of night to the silence comes.
In dream-like state, the shadows play,
Holding on tight to what won't decay.

With every heartbeat, the dusk remains,
A dance of shadows, a woven chain.
In whispers carried on the breeze,
Take heed, dear heart, and learn to seize.

# Whispering Dust in Enchanted Realms

In the forest deep where shadows play,
The dust of whispers guides the way.
Flickering lights in the twilight mist,
Magic unfolds with every tryst.

Underneath the ancient trees,
Secrets carried by the breeze.
Echoing laughter, soft and bright,
Illuminating the tranquil night.

Along the path of silver streams,
Where every stone holds spun-out dreams.
Fae enchantments dance on high,
Glistening like the midnight sky.

In hidden glades where time stands still,
The heart of nature seeks to thrill.
Each rustle tells a tale of old,
In enchanted realms, mysteries unfold.

With every step the world awakes,
In the embrace, our spirit shakes.
Unity in this sacred trust,
Together we become the dust.

# Echoes of Stardust in Shadowed Glades

Beneath the canopy of whispered stars,
The echoes lead us near and far.
Gentle ripples on the darkened lake,
Cradle dreams that shimmer and quake.

In shadowed glades with secrets spun,
The night reveals what's lost in sun.
Faint glimmers brush against the night,
Paint the silence with purest light.

Each sigh of wind, a song of old,
Where stories are in shadows told.
As starlit fragments kiss the ground,
In their embrace, we are spellbound.

Between the moss and ancient stone,
Whispers linger, deep and sown.
Every rustle a softly murmured plea,
In shadowed glades, we come to see.

With every breath, the stardust calls,
Falling gently as evening falls.
In these echoes, hearts ignite,
Guided by the celestial light.

# Luminous Shards Beneath Celestial Canopies

Where the night sky meets the trees,
Luminous shards dance with ease.
Fragments of dreams lost in the flow,
Underneath where wild things grow.

In twilight whispers, worlds align,
Stars emerge like glistening wine.
The sky's embrace, a velvet shroud,
Filling hearts with hope, unbowed.

Among the leaves a shimmer glows,
Illuminating the path we chose.
Every shimmer, a gentle guide,
In celestial canopies, we abide.

With every twinkle, secrets shine,
Threads of fate in the cosmic design.
Each luminous shard a hope repressed,
Reminds us that we're truly blessed.

As the dawn beckons, shadows wane,
In our souls, remains the gain.
Beneath the vast and endless skies,
The luminous shards forever rise.

# Fractured Dreams in Twilight Meadows

In twilight meadows where wishes lie,
Fractured dreams beneath the sky.
Each blade of grass holds tales untold,
Whispers of the young and old.

Silhouettes dance in fading light,
Chasing fragments of pure delight.
In the hush, the magic flows,
In every corner, mystery grows.

Beneath the stars, our hopes take flight,
Painting dreams on the canvas of night.
The air is thick with longing sighs,
As every heartbeat softly tries.

In the fields where shadows blend,
Every vision seems to mend.
Twilight cradles what we seek,
In the silence, spirits speak.

When morning breaks, we'll hold it tight,
The promise of the coming light.
Though dreams may fracture, hope remains,
In twilight meadows, love sustains.

## The Radiant Dust of Forgotten Realms

In the quiet of the night, we wander,
Among the echoes of long-lost dreams.
Stars above whisper secrets yonder,
Guiding us through celestial streams.

Grains of time slip through our fingers,
Carrying tales of those before.
In every shadow, a memory lingers,
A realm where forgotten hearts soar.

The soft glow of twilight enchants,
Painting our paths with hues of gold.
Each step forward, the past grants,
Its wisdom cherished, its stories told.

Faded maps lead to hidden glades,
Where ancient sighs still softly hum.
Among the ruins, legacy wades,
In silent dreams, we find our home.

With each breath, the magic stirs,
Awakening worlds once lost in time.
In radiant dust, our journey blurs,
Transforming hope into sacred rhyme.

# Glimmers of Twilight's Remains

Beneath the veil of twilight's grace,
Soft whispers dance upon the air.
Each fading light leaves a trace,
Of love and loss, beyond compare.

Shadows lengthen, secrets grow,
As day surrenders to the night.
In this moment, hearts overflow,
With dreams that shimmer, pure and bright.

The horizon blushes, a canvas wide,
Where hopes ignite with each new star.
In this quiet hour, we confide,
In glimmers of what we are.

Time stands still, as echoes play,
In the symphony of dusk's embrace.
We gather the remnants of the day,
Each laugh and tear, a cherished trace.

In twilight's arms, we find our peace,
A gentle pause before the dawn.
In these glimmers, our souls release,
As night unfolds, and dreams are drawn.

## Fractured Wishes Beneath the Moon

Underneath the silver glow,
Where dreams collide and wishes break.
In whispered moments, hearts bestow,
The silent hopes we dare to stake.

Fragments of what could have been,
Scattered like leaves in autumn's air.
Each fractured wish, a somber sheen,
A longing held, a whispered prayer.

The moonlight weaves through branches sighing,
Casting shadows on secret streams.
In the night, our souls are trying,
To mend the gaps within our dreams.

In the stillness, emotions swirl,
A dance of light, a haunting song.
Beneath the stars, our thoughts unfurl,
In the embrace of night, we belong.

From broken pieces, we find our truth,
In the glow of the vast unknown.
Fractured wishes guide our youth,
To the paths that lead us home.

# Ethereal Ashes in the Glade

In the heart of the whispering wood,
Where ancient spirits softly dwell,
Ethereal ashes linger, stood,
In quiet reverie, tales to tell.

The air is thick with memories old,
Each gust carries the weight of time.
In twilight's embrace, stories unfold,
A tapestry woven with love and rhyme.

Through the glade, a gentle breeze sways,
Caressing each leaf, each weary tree.
In the stillness, the past plays,
An echo of what used to be.

Fleeting moments in the amber light,
Illuminate paths we once knew.
In the shadows, the lost take flight,
On ethereal wings, forever true.

From the ashes, new life ascends,
As dawn breaks o'er the tranquil land.
In the glade, where time transcends,
We find the beauty of what we planned.

# Glinting Secrets in the Night's Embrace

In shadows deep, the stars do wink,
Whispering stories we dare not think.
Moonlight dances on the brook,
Filling the night with a silver book.

Silent echoes ride the breeze,
Carrying secrets through the trees.
Softly, the world holds its breath tight,
As dreams flicker in the soft twilight.

Luna's glow wraps the earth in delight,
Magic woven through the fabric of night.
Each glint a promise, each twinkle a chance,
In the cosmic embrace, we weave our dance.

Time stands still in this tranquil space,
Bathed in the warmth of the moon's grace.
Whispers of ages forgotten and new,
Unravel the dreams that the darkness drew.

In every shadow, a tale awaits,
Held in the heart of the night's gates.
Glinting secrets, forever concealed,
In the night's embrace, our fates are revealed.

## Ghostly Whispers in Enchanted Silence

In stillness deep, the echoes call,
Haunting melodies, a gentle thrall.
Veils of mist swirl in moon's soft light,
Carrying whispers of forgotten night.

Shadows waltz where the spirits tread,
Chasing stories, both lost and dead.
The woods breathe life to tales untold,
In their embrace, the past unfolds.

Silent moments stretch like time,
Carved in memories, sublime rhyme.
Each rustle holds a ghostly sigh,
Fleeting glimpses of days gone by.

Ancient trees listen with their bark,
To secrets shared in the lonely dark.
They hold the echoes, they guard the dreams,
In enchanted silence, nothing is as it seems.

A world between the realms we walk,
Where phantoms linger and shadows talk.
In the hush, we find our way,
Ghostly whispers guide our stay.

# Timeless Specks in the Realm of Dreams

Across the canvas of slumber's embrace,
Timeless specks dance in sacred space.
Fleeting moments suspended in flight,
As we wander through realms of light.

Stars shimmer softly, a lullaby's hum,
Calling us home to the dreams to come.
With each breath, we drift and sway,
In the tapestry woven, we lose our way.

Polished wishes like crystals gleam,
Reflecting lives in the fabric of dreams.
Time dissolves as we float and glide,
In the realm where our hopes abide.

Every dream a story, each sigh a thread,
Weaving the tales of the life we've led.
In the quiet hours before dawn's light,
The timeless specks shine ever so bright.

Awakening whispers, a new day's song,
Carry the magic where we belong.
In the realm of dreams, we forever roam,
Crafting the essence of our own home.

# Splintered Vows Beneath the Ancient Trees

In the forest deep, where the ancients stand,
Vows were spoken, pure and unplanned.
Roots intertwine, like hearts in embrace,
Splintered whispers of love's gentle grace.

The leaves bear witness to promises made,
In the dappled light where shadows fade.
Time flows like water over smooth stone,
Carrying echoes of love's sweet tone.

Branches stretch high, touch the azure sky,
Guardians of secrets that flutter by.
In each rustle, a memory sings,
Of splintered vows and the joy it brings.

With every season, the stories renew,
In the heart of the forest, love's tribute true.
A sanctuary where souls find peace,
Under the ancient trees, our hearts release.

Forever entwined within nature's keep,
Among the whispers, our promises seep.
In the embrace of the woods, life starts,
Splintered vows live on in our hearts.

# Fragments of Twilight in Moonlit Hollow

In shadows deep where whispers play,
The moonlight spills a silver ray.
A breeze that carries tales of old,
In twilight's grasp, their secrets told.

Beneath the boughs, the starlit skies,
The echoes of forgotten sighs.
Each fragment glows, a fleeting dream,
In hollowed night, all things redeem.

A crystal brook, its waters gleam,
Reflecting every passing beam.
With rustling leaves in soft embrace,
The beauty of this sacred space.

The fireflies dance with gentle grace,
While shadows weave a soft embrace.
In moonlit hollow, still and bright,
Fragments of twilight hold me tight.

As night descends with tender care,
Each whisper fades, a silent prayer.
Among the stars, I find my peace,
In twilight's arms, my heart's release.

# Secrets of the Veil in Enchanted Groves

In enchanted groves where time stands still,
A veil of magic, a soft, sweet thrill.
With ancient trees that softly sigh,
Their secrets held beneath the sky.

The whispering winds sing lullabies,
To hidden hearts and watchful eyes.
Through tangled roots, the stories weave,
In every shadow, we believe.

A carpet bright of emerald green,
Where faeries dance and dreams convene.
The pulse of life, a gentle thrum,
In glowing dusk, our spirits hum.

With every step, the magic grows,
In the twilight's glow, the wonder flows.
Each secret shared, a bond we build,
In enchanted groves, our hearts are filled.

As twilight fades and stars ignite,
The veil lifts slowly, granting light.
In solemn moments, truth will shine,
In nature's grasp, our souls align.

# Shimmering Traces of Lost Light

Upon the field where day meets night,
Shimmering traces of lost light.
Once blazing flames that grace the sky,
Now whispers where the shadows lie.

Glimmers dance on dewy grass,
Echoes of moments, swift to pass.
Memories like fireflies dart,
Illuminating the tender heart.

In twilight's hold, the colors blend,
As daylight's glow begins to end.
Softly fading, yet shining bright,
Shimmering traces weave the night.

The songs of dusk, a lullaby,
To carry dreams through the night sky.
In every breath, a spark ignites,
In shimmering traces, we find light.

With every heartbeat, moments gleam,
Reflecting hopes, a gentle dream.
In twilight's arms, our shadows play,
Shimmering traces guide our way.

## The Dance of Embers in Ethereal Woods

In ethereal woods where silence reigns,
The dance of embers, a soft refrain.
Flickering flames in twilight's embrace,
Illuminate shadows with gentle grace.

Among the trees, the whispers call,
A symphony sweet, enchanting all.
With every flicker, secrets bloom,
In the heart of the forest's room.

Soft wisps of smoke curl into the night,
As stars awaken, a wondrous sight.
The embers pulse with life anew,
In the silence, we are two.

Together we weave through the mystic trees,
Carried along by the autumn breeze.
Where shadows play and dreams align,
The dance of embers, forever mine.

As darkness falls, a tranquil bliss,
In these woods, I find my kiss.
With every heartbeat, stories blend,
In the dance of embers, love shall mend.

# Memories Wrapped in the Fog of Day

In whispers soft, the dawn does break,
Echoes linger, each choice we make.
Fingers trace the misty air,
Lost in thoughts, a silent prayer.

Through shadows dance the fleeting past,
A tapestry too rich to last.
Moments blend with morning light,
Wrapped in dreams, we take our flight.

Veils of time, they curl and sway,
Carrying glimpses of yesterday.
Voices fade, but feelings stay,
In the fog, we find our way.

With every step on dew-kissed grass,
We find the strength to let time pass.
Heartbeats echo, softly call,
In the mist, we rise, we fall.

So here we stand, in silence deep,
Holding memories we wish to keep.
Wrapped in fog, we find our peace,
In fleeting moments, love's release.

# Celestial Glances Over Wistful Horizons

Stars awaken, night takes flight,
Glimmers bright in velvet night.
Horizons stretch with colors bold,
Stories whispered, dreams unfold.

Moonlight bathes the earth below,
Guiding hearts where whispers flow.
Time suspended, hearts ignite,
In the dark, we find our light.

Wistful glances, eyes collide,
In celestial realms, we bide.
Each flicker brings a sweet embrace,
In the heavens, we find our place.

With every sigh, we touch the stars,
Fates entwined, no distance far.
Over cosmic seas we sail,
In shared breaths, our love won't fail.

So let the night draw close and warm,
Under constellations, we transform.
Together, we chase the dawn,
In the beauty of night, we're reborn.

# Fragmented Hearts in Sylvan Shadows

In the woods where silence reigns,
Hearts are mended, held in chains.
Fragmented hopes, like leaves, fall down,
Lost in shadows, none to crown.

Nature wraps us, soft and kind,
Whispers echo, hearts aligned.
Among the trees, we seek to find,
Pieces of love we left behind.

Sunlight dances through the boughs,
Revealing scars, unbroken vows.
In fragmented paths, we tread anew,
Where sylvan shades still speak the truth.

Time and whispers guide our quest,
In nature's arms, we find our rest.
Hearts once shattered, begin to heal,
In the forest, we learn to feel.

So let us wander, hand in hand,
In the shadows, where dreams expand.
Together, we'll make a brand-new start,
In the silence, we'll mend our hearts.

# Shimmering Secrets Under Dusty Moons

Underneath a dusty moon,
Shadows cast a secret tune.
Each shimmer tells a tale untold,
Whispers wrapped in silver gold.

Midnight breezes carry sighs,
Underneath the endless skies.
Dreamers chase the fading light,
With every twinkle, hearts take flight.

Secrets bloom in evening's hush,
A fleeting moment, a gentle rush.
Through the dark, our wishes soar,
In this place, we search for more.

Stars aligned, their glow revealed,
In the night, our souls are healed.
Dusty moons hold timeless dreams,
Stitching fate with gentle seams.

So let us weave our stories right,
In the shadows of the night.
Shimmering dreams and secrets shared,
In dusty moons, our hearts are bared.

# Flickers of Enchantment on Fractured Paths

In the twilight's soft glow, whispers sigh,
Shadows dance lightly, as fireflies fly.
Cracked earth beneath, a secret path we tread,
With each step forward, old legends are fed.

Lost in the woodland where echoes play,
Entwined in the branches, magic holds sway.
Glimmers of hope weave through the trees,
A tapestry spun by the gentlest breeze.

Moss carpets the ground, a cushion so fine,
While starlight above begins to entwine.
Footprints of dreamers, etched in the night,
Guide us through shadows to find hidden light.

Each rustling leaf tells a tale long untold,
Of sprites and of whispers, and fables of old.
The path unfolds mysteries, thick with allure,
Beckoning hearts through the enchanting obscure.

With wishes unspoken, we follow our guide,
Into realms where the magical reside.
Flickers of enchantment, so vivid and bright,
Lead us through darkness into the light.

# The Silence of Dreams Beneath the Stars

In the hush of the night, when the world's at rest,
Whispers of dreams curl, like tendrils caressed.
Beneath the vast sky where the starlight beams,
We wander through shadows, tracing our dreams.

Glimmers of hope in the depth of the void,
The silence of night softly comes to avoid.
With every heartbeat, the cosmos unfolds,
A story of wonders and secrets untold.

Each twinkling star is a wish from afar,
Carrying visions, guiding souls like a star.
In this tranquil realm where time stands still,
The dreams that we harbor begin to fulfill.

So close your eyes gently, embrace the unknown,
Let silence envelop, let your spirit be sown.
For beneath the bright sheen of celestial charms,
The silence of dreams holds you in its arms.

With wishes woven in stardust and glee,
We write our own fables, a tale to decree.
In the silence of dreams, beneath endless skies,
We rise with the dawn, with a new set of eyes.

## Splintered Light in the Fae's Embrace

In the glen where the wildflowers sway,
Splintered light dances through night and day.
The fae cradle secrets in shimmering hands,
As laughter and whispers weave through the lands.

Underneath boughs where the shadows entwine,
A world filled with wonders, both yours and mine.
Each flicker of glory, a tale to unveil,
In the heart of the forest, on soft, mossy trail.

Dreams waltz on petals, in soft, gentle flight,
As splintered light glimmers, so pure and so bright.
Embraced by the magic, we feel ourselves soar,
In the realm of the fae, we forget evermore.

The songs of the ancients, carried by breeze,
Not confined to silence, they rustle with ease.
In each sigh of the earth, a resonant call,
A summoning deep, pulling us into thrall.

As dusk begins painting its velvety hue,
We dance in the twilight where dreams slip anew.
With splintered light surrounding, our hearts find their
grace,
In the boundless embrace of the fae's gentle space.

# Echoes of Magic in Natural Cradles

In the quietest corners where nature resides,
Echoes of magic flow like gentle tides.
Between the soft whispers of leaves up above,
Lies a cradle of wonders, a sanctuary of love.

With every heartbeat, the earth sings its song,
A melody woven, where souls feel they belong.
In the rustling ferns and the babbling brook,
We find echoes of magic in every nook.

As sunlight is filtered through emerald trees,
Nature's embrace wraps us, calming our pleas.
With each tender breath, we feel life anew,
In the cradle of whispers, our spirits break through.

The laughter of streams and the call of the dove,
Unites every creature in a symphony of love.
In the depths of the forest or the wide open skies,
Magic is pregnant, waiting to rise.

With each step we take, we awaken the dreams,
That linger and shimmer, like cool silver streams.
Through echoes of magic, may our hearts entwine,
In natural cradles, where stars forever shine.

# Illuminated Secrets of the Silent Night

In velvet skies, the stars align,
Whispers of dreams in soft design.
Moonlight dances on quiet streams,
Unveiling the secrets of starlit themes.

Resting in shadows, the world takes pause,
While mysteries linger without a cause.
Nature breathes slow, in tranquil delight,
Holding the echoes of the night.

Silent wisdom in flickering rays,
Guiding the heart through endless maze.
Each twinkling light tells a story untold,
In the soft darkness, the night unfolds.

Glimmers of hope in the cool night air,
A calm assurance, a tender flare.
Illuminated secrets beckon close,
Inviting the soul to wander, to rose.

In the embrace of the serene dark,
Stars ignite dreams, a luminous spark.
The night hums low, a calming song,
In its quietude, we belong.

# Celestial Blooms Hidden in Twilight's Embrace

Petals unfurling in evening's glow,
Secrets held where soft breezes blow.
Colors bleed into the dusky sky,
A canvas alive as day says goodbye.

Moonlit gardens whisper their names,
As twilight cloaks them in gentle flames.
Celestial blooms, in fragrant delight,
Reside in the magic of coming night.

Stars emerge as blossoms of light,
Painting the heavens, a wondrous sight.
Nestled in shadows, the miracles grow,
In twilight's embrace, we begin to know.

Softly they nod in the breezy air,
Moments of beauty, tender and rare.
Twilight's embrace, a magical trance,
Invites us to ponder, invites us to dance.

Beneath the veil of the waning day,
Celestial blooms beckon, guiding our way.
In fragrant nocturnes, our spirits entwine,
With each gentle sigh, their essence divine.

# Fragments of Luminescence in Mystic Spheres

In the cosmos, fragments of light,
Dance through the shadows, brilliant and bright.
Mystic spheres hold tales of the past,
Echoing whispers of shadows cast.

Luminous clusters weave tales of time,
In galaxies vast, a celestial rhyme.
Each twinkle holds dreams waiting to soar,
Fragments of wonder forevermore.

Boundless realms of glowing delight,
Shimmer with secrets from depths of night.
In the heart of darkness, stories entwine,
Fragments of luminescence, forever shine.

Journey through orbs both heavy and light,
Chasing the fragments, igniting the night.
Mystic adventures in cosmic art,
Awaken the dreams buried in the heart.

Stars bear witness to the pain and joy,
Softly illuminating the dreams we deploy.
In each twinkle, a universe is born,
Fragments of light, eternally worn.

## Flickering Glimpses of Forgotten Lore

Flickering flames tell stories of old,
In the heart of the night, their tales unfold.
Glances of wisdom in each tiny spark,
Resurrecting tales lost in the dark.

Whispers of ancients drift through the air,
Echoing softly, like a lover's prayer.
Forgotten lore dances in shadows' embrace,
Illuminating paths through time and space.

Glimmers of truth linger on the tongue,
In the flickering light, the heart's songs are sung.
History pulses in each crackling sound,
As wisdom of ages gathers around.

Through the haze of the memory's glow,
Stories emerge, both healing and slow.
Flickering glimpses of what once was bright,
Guide us from shadows into the light.

So gather the echoes, heed the night's call,
For moments of magic reside over all.
In flickering glances, we honor the lore,
A legacy cherished forevermore.

# Shining Dust in Enchanted Realms

In fields where starlight softly, gleams,
The whispers dance in moonlit beams.
Each glinting speck a story told,
Of magic realms in dreams of gold.

Beneath the trees, in twilight's glow,
The shimmering dust begins to flow.
Enchantments linger in the air,
Awakening secrets everywhere.

Together, creatures twirl and spin,
As shadows weave the tales within.
A gentle breeze calls forth the night,
Embracing all in soft delight.

In this realm where fantasy plays,
The heart ignites in wild arrays.
Elysian echoes, pure and bright,
Illuminate the velvet night.

So let us wander, hand in hand,
Through shining spaces, free and grand.
With every step, our spirits soar,
In enchanted realms forevermore.

# Crumbling Wishes Wrapped in Faerie Breath

In gardens filled with petals pale,
Crumbling wishes on the trail.
Each sigh a promise lost in time,
Wrapped in faerie breath, a rhyme.

Whispers drift on winds that roam,
Carrying dreams that seek a home.
Each star a light, a glinting hope,
In shadows where the fairies cope.

Through twilight's haze, the magic flows,
As twilight's blush on silence grows.
A fleeting glance, a broken kiss,
In every moment, echoes twist.

Yet hope takes root in gentle care,
In every nook, in every prayer.
The crumbling wishes rise anew,
In faerie breath, our dreams break through.

So softly weave the threads of night,
With every wish, we take to flight.
In crumbling hopes, we find our way,
Wrapped in magic, come what may.

# The Whisper of Shadows in the Moon's Grip

The whisper of shadows softly sings,
In the quiet where the nightingale swings.
Moonlight drapes its silver lace,
Wrapping all in a gentle embrace.

Each flicker dances near the ground,
Where secrets of the dark abound.
A ghostly sigh through the midnight air,
Crafting dreams with an evanescent flair.

Listen close, as the dark unveils,
Stories woven in softest trails.
The moon's grip pulls the heart and mind,
To hidden worlds, where hopes are twined.

A rustle stirs the ancient trees,
Bringing forth a whispering breeze.
In shadows deep, the echoes glide,
Where mysteries and wonders hide.

So wander forth, beneath the sky,
Let every shadow draw you nigh.
In the moon's grip, gently tread,
Where whispers linger, dreams are fed.

# Glinting Paths in Ethereal Dreams

Upon the hills where starlight sighs,
Glinting paths draw forth surprise.
A trail of wonders leading deep,
Where ethereal dreams softly creep.

Each step a dance, a fleeting trace,
In a realm that time cannot erase.
The night unfolds its velvet cloak,
In glimmers bright, the heart awoke.

As silver streams through valleys flow,
With every glint, new worlds bestow.
In dreams we chase the shining light,
Through whispers sweet in the hush of night.

So let us wander, hand in hand,
Together in this wonderland.
With every heartbeat, we perceive,
The magic that we choose to weave.

In glinting paths, where dreams reside,
Our spirits soar, our souls abide.
With starlit skies our guiding beams,
We dance along ethereal dreams.